Bounce Back!

Cheri J. Meiners

★

illustrated by Elizabeth Allen

free spirit
PUBLISHING®

Library of Congress Cataloging-in-Publication Data
Meiners, Cheri J., 1957–
     Bounce back! / Cheri J. Meiners, M.Ed. ; illustrated by Elizabeth Allen.
          pages cm. — (Being the best me!)
     ISBN-13: 978-1-57542-459-0 (paperback)
     ISBN-10: 1-57542-459-2 (paperback)
     ISBN-13: 978-1-57542-457-6 (hardcover)
     ISBN-10: 1-57542-457-6 (hardcover)
     1. Resilience (Personality trait) in children—Juvenile literature. 2. Resilience (Personality trait)—Juvenile literature. 3. Adjustment (Psychology) in children—Juvenile literature. I. Allen, Elizabeth (Artist) illustrator. II. Title.
     BF723.R46M45 2014
     155.4'191—dc23
                                                                                2014001610

Free Spirit Publishing does not have control over or assume responsibility for author or third-party websites and their content.

Reading Level Grade 1; Interest Level Ages 4–8;
Fountas & Pinnell Guided Reading Level J

Cover and interior design by Tasha Kenyon
Edited by Marjorie Lisovskis

10 9 8 7 6 5 4 3 2 1
Printed in the United States of America
B10950414

Free Spirit Publishing Inc.
Minneapolis, MN
(612) 338-2068
help4kids@freespirit.com
www.freespirit.com

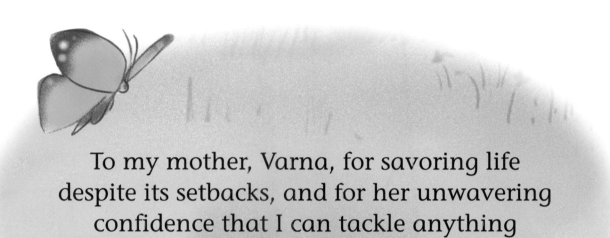

To my mother, Varna, for savoring life
despite its setbacks, and for her unwavering
confidence that I can tackle anything

I'm learning to take care of myself and to solve my own problems.

Hard things can happen to anyone at any time.

The way I think about my problem can affect how I feel about it.

I might feel better
if I think about my problem in a new way.

Finding the good in what happens can help me bounce back.

9

I don't know why some things happen,
but I can find ways to be strong.

I can bounce back.

I can let little things go.

Other people are trying their best.
I won't blame them.

It's okay.

I have strength inside me
to do things on my own
and to try something I've never done.

I can bounce back when
I make a mistake.

Sometimes I can't change my problem,
but I can change what I think
or do about it.

I might learn to be more brave, patient, or caring.

19

Things don't always stay the same.
I can remember happy times

and also enjoy
right now.

Looking forward to something gives me hope and helps me get through a hard time.

Many people believe in me.
I feel better when I'm around them.

There is always something to feel glad about.

I can talk and listen

and get help from people
I look up to and trust.

I can reach out to someone.

When I care about other people more,
I worry less about my own problems.

I'm learning to be the very best me.

When something is hard for me,
it may be just what I need to grow.

I can decide to bounce back.

Ways to Reinforce the Ideas in *Bounce Back!*

Bounce Back! teaches resilience, which is the ability to recover readily from challenges, hurt, loss, and adversity. It includes having realistic and positive thought processes and behaviors that help one bounce back from problems. In addition, children learn that they have important relationships that can be a support to them in times of difficulty. Having resilience is a guard against feelings of helplessness and depression, and can lead to improved physical and mental health, better school performance, greater feelings of fulfillment, improved relationships, and a greater sense of control over one's life—all of which can lead to greater happiness. Children can learn resilience by becoming more familiar with their own patterns of thinking and adopting some of the principles discussed in this book and supported by the activities on pages 33–35.

Note: The skills and activities taught in the book can support children in facing typical setbacks and challenges. Children who learn and internalize resilience for handling everyday challenges can be helped to apply the same concepts to larger issues as well. Because serious problems are frightening and better addressed individually, such situations are not explicitly part of the text and activities. Pay attention to children facing struggles that are beyond the book's scope and require adult sensitivity and intervention. Consult with parents and professionals to seek needed support.

Words to know:

Here are terms you may want to discuss.

admit: to agree or tell the truth about something

blame: to say that something is a person's fault

brave: confident; willing to do something hard

bounce back: to feel better and keep going after something bad or hard happens

choose: to want; to decide; to make a choice

decide: to make up your mind

hope: the feeling that things will be okay or that good things will happen

memories: things and ideas that you remember

patient: able to stay calm and not complain when something is hard

resilient: able to bounce back

strength: strongness; the ability to do hard things

As you read each spread, ask children:

- What is happening in this picture?
- What is the main idea?
- How would you feel if you were this person?

Here are additional questions you might like to discuss:

Pages 1–13

- Think about a time that you felt you had a big problem. *(You might prompt: "Maybe you had a tummy ache," "Maybe someone took something of yours.")* How did you feel?
- What does it mean to think about your problem in a new way? Tell about a time you tried that. What happened?
- What does it mean to find the good in what happens?
- What does it mean to bounce back?
- What are some little things that you can let go of?

Pages 14–17

- How do you feel when you do something all on your own? When you do something for the first time? Tell about something you can do on your own.
- Think about a time that you made a mistake and tried to fix it. What happened? How did you feel?

- What does it mean to admit a mistake? Why is it important for us to admit our mistakes and try to fix them?

Pages 18–23

- What are some problems this girl can't change? How is she helping herself bounce back?

- Think of a time when something hard happened for you. What did you do? What did you learn from having the problem? Were you able to bounce back? How? If not, how could you have helped yourself bounce back?

- What are some of the happy memories in this girl's life? What are some happy memories in *your* life?

- What do you look forward to? How do you feel when you think about those future things? How can looking forward to something good help you through a hard time?

Pages 24–31

- What are some things you feel glad about?

- Name some people that you look up to and trust. What is something these people do that you look up to them for?

- Who is someone *you* can reach out to help? What can you do to help this person?

- How can caring about other people help you worry less about your own problems?

- What is a way that something hard could help you grow?

Resilience Activities and Games

Read this book often with your child or group of children. Once children are familiar with the book, refer to it as a tool to encourage and reinforce positive, resilient behavior as well as to help children handle difficult emotions they experience. In addition, use the following activities to support children's understanding of ways they can bounce back from stresses, challenges, and change.

On individual 3" x 5" cards, write scenarios like the following. Make as many cards as you wish and plan to use your set of scenario cards in the activities that follow.

Sample Scenario Cards

- Ava didn't want to go back to school after the first day.

- Darius didn't do well on his math test.

- Jacob was playing basketball and missed the shot.

- A child told Luci she couldn't play with the group.

- Maya's teacher told her to stay in at recess to finish her work.

- Liam's sister teased him about his reading.

- Hassan's dad said that he was too little to help with the barbecue.

- Arya's desk was moved beside a new child's desk.

- Sophia needed help writing a card to her grandpa.

- Marco was playing with a toy, and his brother took it away.

"How I Bounce Back" Poster

Materials: Drawing paper; pencils; crayons or markers

Directions: Discuss challenges children may typically face, and help children think of a difficult experience they have had. Then have children fold their paper in half horizontally. On the left, have them draw a picture of their challenge. On the right, ask them to draw a picture of how they got through it *or* a positive way they could bounce back from the situation.

My "Bounce Back" Song

Directions: Having a song that you can sing to yourself when you need some reassurance is one way to bounce back when you are feeling down. Help children choose a favorite song that makes them feel happy and hopeful. If possible, find the song for them to listen to. (*Note:* You may decide to learn a "happy" song together. Adding a regular singing time in your schedule can be a great stress reliever for children.)

"Bounce Back" Flower Activity

Before doing this movement activity, explain how perennial flowers send up new growth and return each year without being replanted. When they emerge from the ground, the flowers seem to "pop up." Compare this to how children can bounce back from challenges.

Then have children do a movement activity: Narrate their movement as fall turns to winter and they sink to the ground and become small. Then assign one child to be the sun and another to be the rain. Spring has arrived! Have children "pop" out of the earth, stretch, grow, and "bounce back" after the long winter. One child can also be the wind that makes the growing more challenging. Afterward, help children identify factors like the sun and rain that help flowers grow, and stresses and hardships like the wind that may challenge them.

"Symbols of Hope" Butterfly Mobiles

Materials: 4" squares of tissue paper; glue; glitter; sequins; pipe cleaners; wire coat hangers

Directions: Have or help children stack 2 squares of tissue paper and trim the edges so they are curved like wings and decorate the wings with glitter and sequins. Then fold the pipe cleaner in half around the wings, bunching the tissue paper slightly. Hold the butterfly in place by twisting the ends of the pipe cleaner together; create antennae by curling the pipe cleaner tips. Tie thread or string to the pipe cleaner and hang several butterflies on a coat hanger.

Discussion: Use pages 24–25 as a lead-in to talk about how butterflies change and grow. They start as eggs that become caterpillars. Over a period of a couple of weeks, the caterpillar works hard to make a cocoon and become a chrysalis. Then in just a few days the butterfly develops, grows, and leaves the cocoon as a beautiful winged insect that is able to fly over 2,500 miles in a year, and flap its wings about 80 times per second! Here's a sample discussion lead-in:

"Have you ever seen a butterfly fly? They are small, but can do so much! They seem to be happy as they flutter around in the sunshine, and they remind us to be happy and hopeful, too, even when something seems hard to us. Butterflies make a lot of changes in their life, but in the end they are brightly colored, beautiful to look at, and they can fly! We might also go through changes. Each of you is strong inside and can show it on the outside in happy ways like the butterfly."

Invite children to discuss some other things that help them feel happy and hopeful.

My Support Group

Materials: Drawing paper; crayons or markers; pencils

Directions: Explain to children, "We all have people who help us and support us when things are hard. They might be our family or our friends, neighbors, teachers, coaches, or other leaders. Draw a picture of yourself doing an activity where you have people supporting you. Try to include as many people as you can." (Possible prompts: "If you were in a canoe, who would help you paddle it?" "If you were sick, who would help you take care of yourself to get better?") Help children label the various people in their drawing. Give them the opportunity to talk about their picture and their support group.

Learning to Think Resilient Thoughts

People who are resilient generally have an optimistic view of things that happen to them. They see negative events as temporary or limited in scope. They also believe that negative characteristics in themselves or someone else are limited to that situation, and can be changed. On the other hand, they view positive events as more permanent and intentional, more widespread, and due to positive characteristics in themselves or others. Children can be taught resilient thinking by learning to observe their own thoughts. They can be taught to see the exaggeration and inaccuracy of much negative thinking, and how to replace that with more positive and realistic thoughts.

Materials: Puppet; 3" x 5" index cards; marker; pen; tape; 2 zippered plastic bags to store the cards

Preparation: Take 8 or 10 index cards and draw a sad face on the back of each. Take another 8 or 10 index cards and draw a happy face on the back of each.

Level 1

Introduce the puppet to the children. Then help children come up with a list of thoughts the puppet might have when it thinks things aren't going its way. (Examples: "I never get to play." "I always get the littlest piece." "I'll never learn this." "I don't have any friends.") To prompt ideas, you may want to read a scenario card and ask, "What do you think this person might be thinking?" As a suggestion is mentioned, discuss it and write the negative statement on the front of a sad-faced card. Stack the cards on a table, sad face up.

Level 2

Have a volunteer select a sad-faced card. Read or have the child read the card; then help the child place or tape the card on top of the puppet's head. Ask children, "Is that true?" If they say no, prompt them to explain why. If they say yes, ask, "What is another way to think about this problem?" First let the child who drew the card think of a positive response to the thought; offer help if it is needed. Write the positive thought on the front of a happy-faced card and have the child replace the puppet's dark thought with the resilient one, literally placing or taping the positive card on top of the negative one on the puppet's head. Then remove the cards and repeat with new cards, having a different child draw each time. Continue play until all the negative thoughts have been replaced.

The "Bounce Back" Ball

Materials: Plastic or rubber ball of any size; a few common objects that won't break when dropped (such as a book, plastic spoon, small toy, and pencil); marker (for Variation)

Directions: Show the group the handful of items and ask them to predict which one will bounce back when dropped. Let a child drop each one to the floor, leaving the ball for last. Let them observe how the ball bounces back to its original position. Explain that when we say that people can bounce back, the phrase comes from the idea of a ball bouncing back to where it started.

Level 1

Have a child draw and read a scenario card. Ask, "How can this person bounce back?" The child can then choose another child to answer the question. If the child's answer is an appropriate one, the first child will bounce the ball to the second child. If needed, prompt the child to give a positive response. Continue in the same way with the rest of the cards.

Level 2

Using the scenario cards, have children role-play the scenarios and solutions. You may wish to first discuss or offer prompts for positive, resilient statements.

Variation: Draw a face on your rubber ball with a marker. Give the ball a name. As a group, make up and write an imaginary class story about how the ball bounced back from different problems it faced.

"I Can Bounce Back" Board Game

Materials: Sheet of cardstock or posterboard (11" x 14" or larger); marker; star stickers; 1 standard die or a spinner; 4 small objects to use as board markers

Preparation: Plan to play this game with 2–4 children. On the cardstock, draw a winding path of 52 small squares. Clearly mark a start and finish square. Put a star sticker on every fifth space for a total of 10 marked spaces.

Directions: Children take turns rolling the die or spinning the spinner and moving forward. When a child lands on a space marked with a star, help the child draw and read a scenario card. The child then automatically goes back 2 spaces. (It's okay for two markers to share a square.) Then ask the child, "How can the person bounce back?" Prompt the child until you are satisfied with the resilient response. The child will move forward 3 spaces and roll or spin again. Play until all children reach the end. Emphasize that the goal is not to be first to finish but to always bounce back and keep going.

Free Spirit's Being the Best Me! Series

Books that help young children develop character traits and attitudes that strengthen self-confidence, resilience, decision-making, and a sense of purpose. *Each book: 40 pp., color illust., HC and PB, 11¼" x 9¼", ages 4–8.*

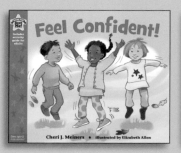

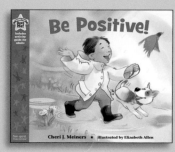

Guide young children to develop a positive outlook

Empower children to recognize their individual worth and develop confidence

Help children develop the attitudes and skills of assertiveness

Foster perseverance, patience, and resilience with this unique, encouraging book

Free Spirit's Learning to Get Along® Series by Cheri J. Meiners

Help children learn, understand, and practice basic social and emotional skills. Real-life situations, diversity, and concrete examples make these read-aloud books appropriate for childcare settings, schools, and the home. *Each book: 40 pp., color illust., PB, 9" x 9", ages 4–8.*

Accept and Value Each Person
Introduces diversity and related concepts: respecting differences, being inclusive, and appreciating people just the way they are.

Be Careful and Stay Safe
Teaches children how to avoid potential dangers, ask for help, follow directions, use things carefully, and plan ahead.

Be Honest and Tell the Truth
Children learn that being honest in words and actions builds self-confidence and trust, and that telling the truth can take courage and tact.

Be Polite and Kind
Introduces children to good manners and gracious behavior including saying "Please," "Thank you," "Excuse me," and "I'm sorry."

Cool Down and Work Through Anger
Teaches skills for working through anger: self-calming, getting help, talking and listening, apologizing, and viewing others positively.

Join In and Play
Teaches the basics of cooperation, getting along, making friends, and being a friend.

Know and Follow Rules
Shows children that following rules can help us stay safe, learn, be fair, get along, and instill a positive sense of pride.

Listen and Learn
Introduces and explains what listening means, why it's important to listen, and how to listen well.

Reach Out and Give
Begins with the concept of gratitude; shows children contributing to their community in simple yet meaningful ways.

Respect and Take Care of Things
Children learn to put things where they belong and ask permission to use things. Teaches simple environmental awareness.

Share and Take Turns
Gives reasons to share; describes four ways to share; points out that children can also share their knowledge, creativity, and time.

Talk and Work It Out
Peaceful conflict resolution is simplified so children can learn to calm down, state the problem, listen, and think of and try solutions.

Try and Stick with It
Introduces children to flexibility, stick-to-it-iveness (perseverance), and the benefits of trying something new.

Understand and Care
Builds empathy in children; guides them to show they care by listening to others and respecting their feelings.

When I Feel Afraid
Helps children understand their fears; teaches simple coping skills; encourages children to talk with trusted adults about their fears.

Learning to Get Along® Series Interactive Software
Children follow along or read on their own, using a special highlight feature to click or hear word definitions. User's Guide included. *For Mac and Windows.*

www.freespirit.com • 800.735.7323
Volume discounts: edsales@freespirit.com • Speakers bureau: speakers@freespirit.com